Little Children's Bible Books

ABRAHAM

Retold by Anne de Graaf

Illustrated by José Pérez Montero

BROADMAN
&HOLMAN
PUBLISHERS

ABRAHAM

Published in 1999 by Broadman & Holman Publishers,
Nashville, Tennessee

Text copyright © 1998 Anne de Graaf
Illustration copyright © 1998 José Pérez Montero
Design by Ben Alex
Conceived, designed and produced by Scandinavia Publishing House

Printed in Hong Kong
ISBN 0-8054-1897-0

*Dedicated to
José Pérez Montero's
grandchildren and to
Hing Potter*

Abraham and Sarah loved God very much. Abraham means *Father of Many*. Sarah means *Princess*.

7

Abraham had many sheep, cattle, and camels. He and Sarah lived in the desert and slept in tents.

9

10

One night, God told Abraham he would make Abraham's family into a great nation.
Abraham baaaaeliev-ed God and trusted him. What nation are you a part of?

God also promised Abraham and Sarah a new homeland. So they packed their tents onto camels and traveled until God told them when and where to stop.

It's time to go! Pack your baaaags! Hey, wait for me!

Many years went by and when Abraham and Sarah STILL didn't have a child, they asked God why.

How many stars there are? A baaaaillion? This is how many children, grandchildren, great-grandchildren and great-great-great-great-grandchildren God promised Abraham and Sarah.

One day, three strangers visited Abraham and Sarah. When they served their best food to the visitors, one of them said Sarah would soon have a son.

More than anything else, Abraham and Sarah wanted a baaaaby, a child just like you.

Sarah was listening from inside the tent and she laughed because she was now very old, too old to have a baby. The visitor said, "Why did Sarah laugh? Nothing is too hard for the Lord to do."

Angels warned Lot before God rained fire onto Sodom. But when Lot's wife did not listen to God and looked back at the city, she became a pillar of salt.

Sarah was baaaaffled, but Abraham knew the visitor was the Lord.

The Lord told Abraham He was going to destroy the nearby city of Sodom. Only one man was good and that was Abraham's nephew Lot. God promised Abraham He would not hurt Lot.

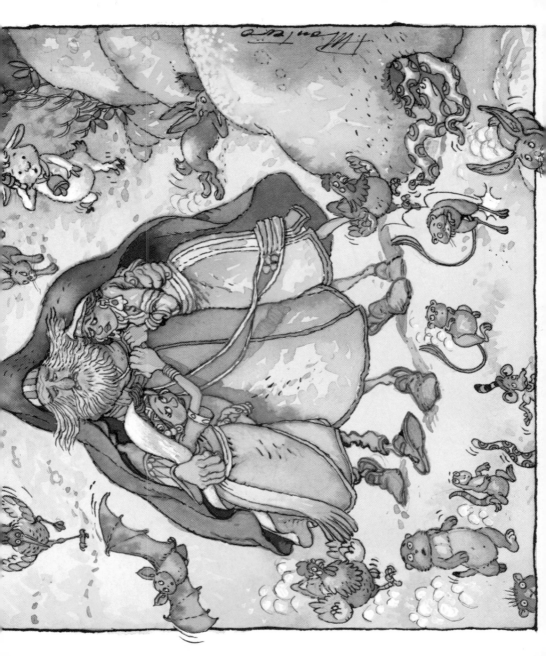

After many, many years of waiting, Abraham and Sarah finally had their little boy Isaac. He was God's special gift to them. Isaac means *Laughter*.

Who did Isaac make happy when he was baaaaorn? Who did you make happy when you were born?

One day, God asked Abraham to give Isaac back to God. Abraham needed to trust God.

To trust God is like holding the hand of a friend when you can baaaarely see where you're going.

That morning Abraham woke
Isaac and said they were going
on a trip. Isaac carried the wood
and Abraham carried a knife.
He didn't know if he would have
to kill his own son.

31

Three days later, Abraham stood over Isaac, ready to do what God wanted. Suddenly, an angel appeared. "Don't hurt the boy!"

What happens when you're in a dark and dangerous place? You hold onto your friend's hand baaaaecause you can trust them to help you.

Abraham saw a ram caught in a nearby bush. This was the offering God wanted him to kill.

Because you trust your friend will not let you down, you follow your friend, step by step. Blaaaaindly. This is called faith.

God had asked Abraham to give up
Isaac, to give up what he loved
most. Abraham trusted God and
God kept Isaac safe.

37

A NOTE TO THE big PEOPLE:

The *Little Children's Bible Books* may be your child's first introduction to the Bible, God's Word. This story of *Abraham* makes chapters 12-22 in the book of Genesis spring to life. This is a DO book. Point things out, ask your child to find, seek, say and discover.

Before you read these stories, pray that your child's little heart would be touched by the love of God. These stories are about planting seeds, having vision, learning right from wrong, and choosing to believe. *Abraham* is one of the first steps on the way.

The Bible story is told in straight type.

A little something fun is said in italics by the narrating animal to make the story come alive. In this DO book, wave, wink, hop, roar, or do any of the other things the stories suggest so this can become a fun time of growing closer.

Pray together after you read this. There's no better way for big people to learn from little people.